POP PIANO HITS

SIMPLE ARRANGEMENTS FOR STUDENTS OF ALL AGES

Adore You, We Are Warriors & More Hot Singles

T0079351

ISBN 978-1-70510-783-6

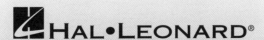

Visit Hal Leonard Online at
www.halleonard.com

Contact us:
Hal Leonard
7777 West Bluemound Road
Milwaukee, WI 53213
Email: info@halleonard.com

In Europe, contact:
Hal Leonard Europe Limited
42 Wigmore Street
Marylebone, London, W1U 2RN
Email: info@halleonardeurope.com

In Australia, contact:
Hal Leonard Australia Pty. Ltd.
4 Lentara Court
Cheltenham, Victoria, 3192 Australia
Email: info@halleonard.com.au

Contents

RAIN ON ME

Words and Music by STEFANI GERMANOTTA,
MARTIN BRESSO, MICHAEL TUCKER,
RAMI YACOUB, ARIANA GRANDE,
NIJA CHARLES, MATTHEW BURNS
and ALEXANDER RIDHA

Upbeat Dance Pop

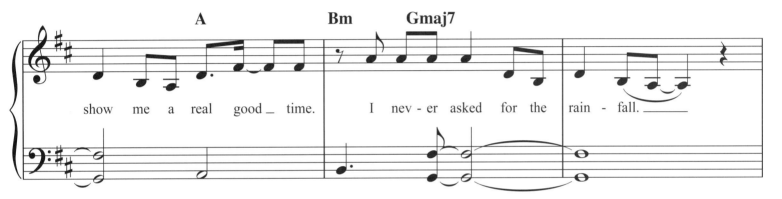

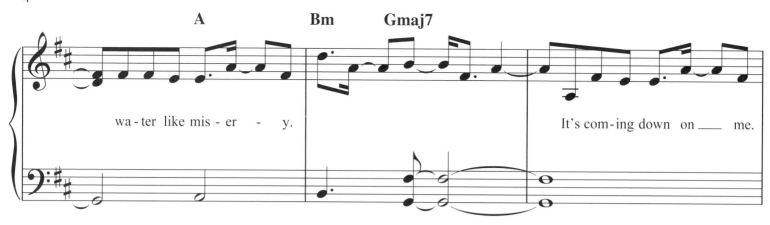

Rain   on   me.

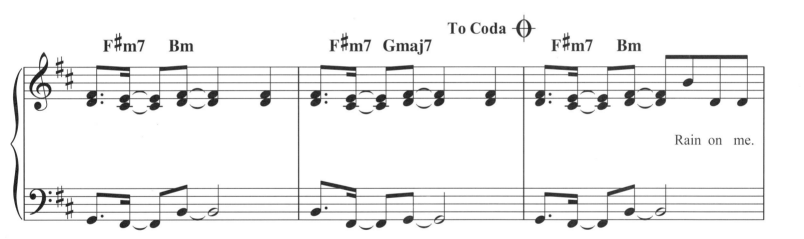

To Coda

Rain on me.

Liv - ing in a world where no one's in - no - cent.

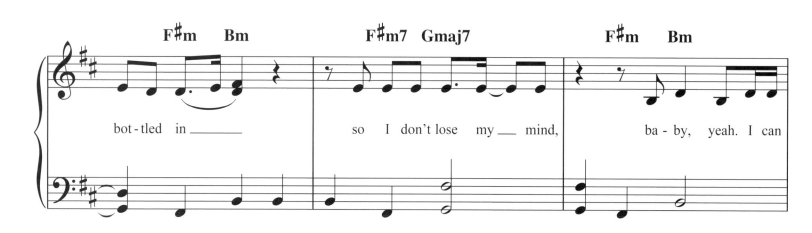

D.S. al Coda

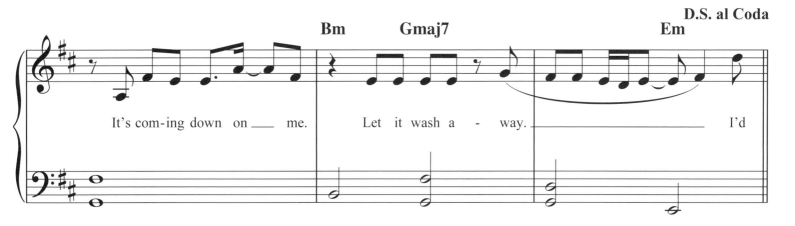

It's com-ing down on ___ me.   Let it wash a - way. _____ I'd

CODA

Rain on me.   Rain on me.

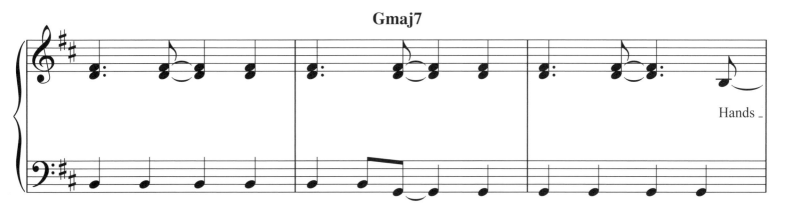

Hands _

___ up to the sky,   I'll be your gal-ax-y. I'm ___ a-bout to fly.

ADORE YOU

Words and Music by HARRY STYLES,
THOMAS HULL, TYLER JOHNSON
and AMY ALLEN

Moderate Pop Rock

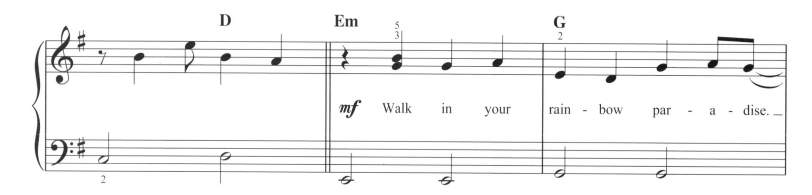

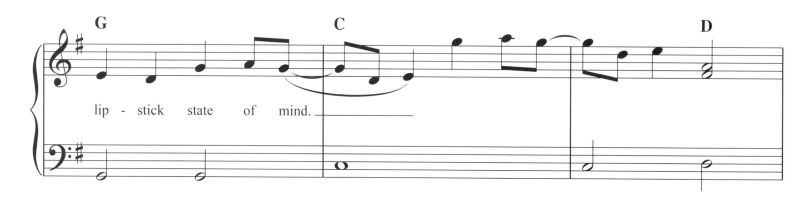

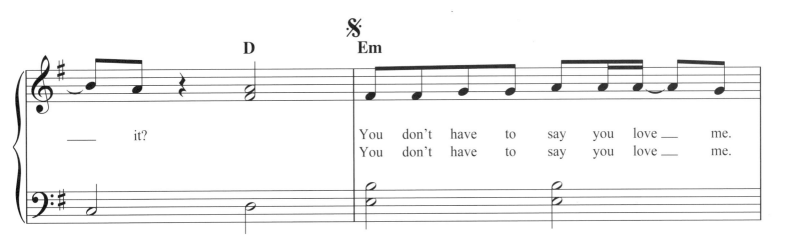

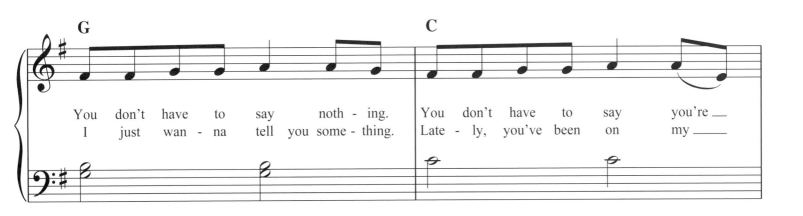

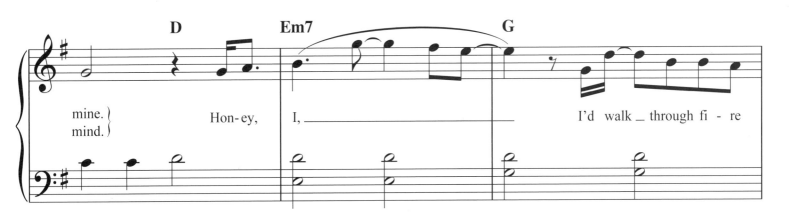

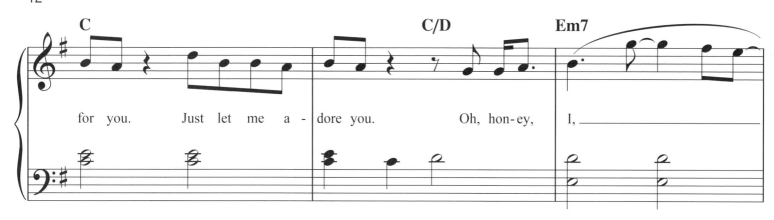

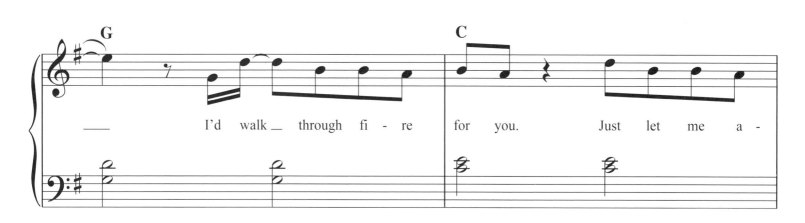

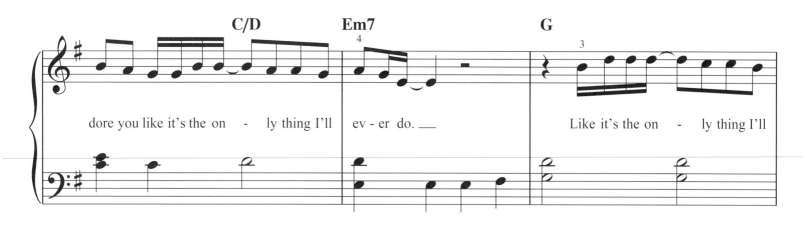

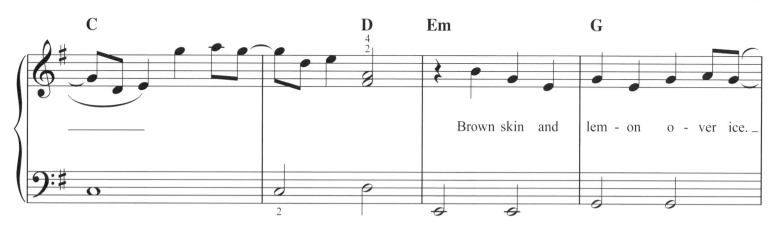

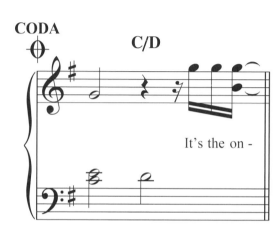

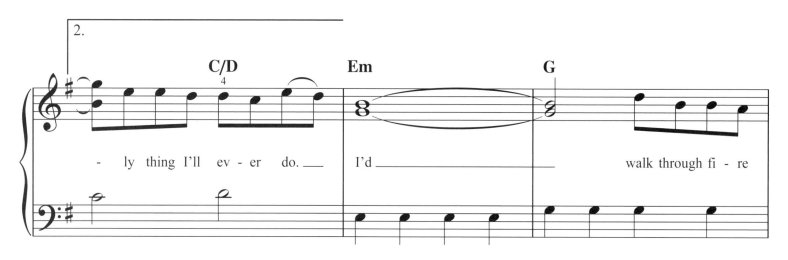

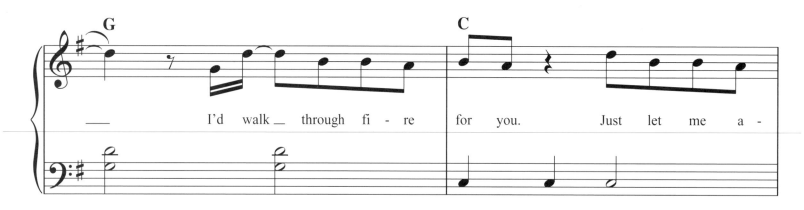

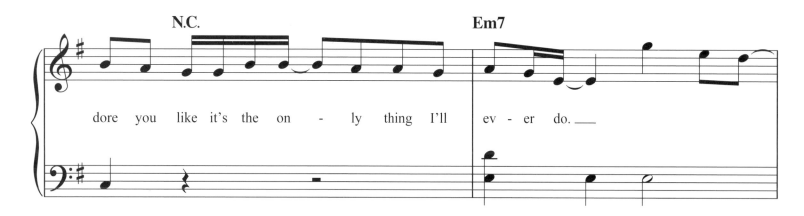

BETTER DAYS

Words and Music by RYAN TEDDER,
BRENT KUTZLE and JOHN NATHANIEL

Oh, I know that there'll be bet - ter days. ___

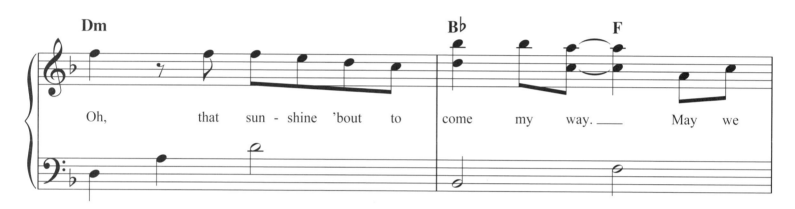

Oh, that sun - shine 'bout to come my way. ___ May we

nev - er, ev - er shed an - oth - er tear for to - day, ___ 'cause,

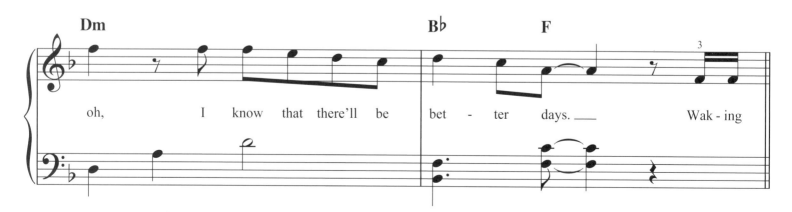

oh, I know that there'll be bet - ter days. ___ Wak - ing

up in Cal - i - for - nia, ___ but these clouds, they won't go a - way. ___ Ev - 'ry
up ___ to a new year; ___ got the past a mil - lion miles a - way. ___ I've been wak - ing

day is like an - oth - er storm, yeah. I'm just try - ing not to go in - sane. ___ In the
up ___ with a new ___ fear, ___ but I know it - 'll wash a - way. ___ What - ev - er you

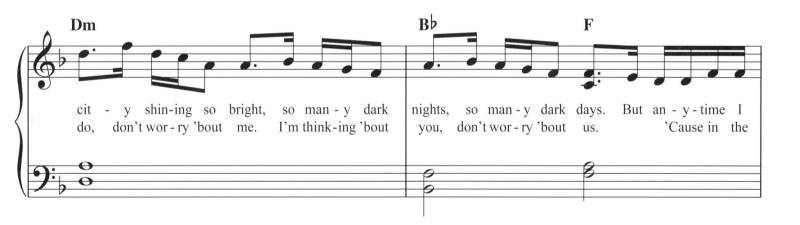

cit - y shin - ing so bright, so man - y dark nights, so man - y dark days. But an - y - time I
do, don't wor - ry 'bout me. I'm think - ing 'bout you, don't wor - ry 'bout us. 'Cause in the

feel the par - a - noi - a, ___ I close my eyes and I pray.
morn - ing, ev - 'ry - thing can change, _ yeah, and time will tell you it does.

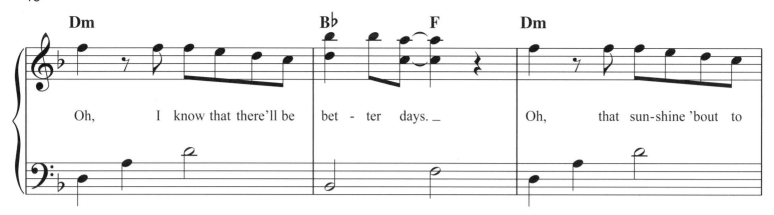

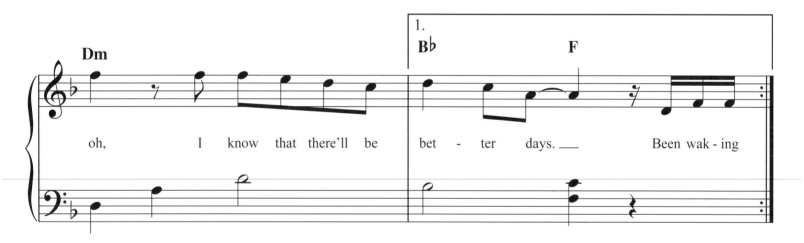

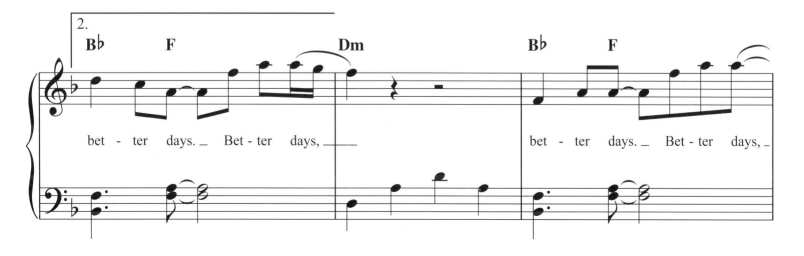

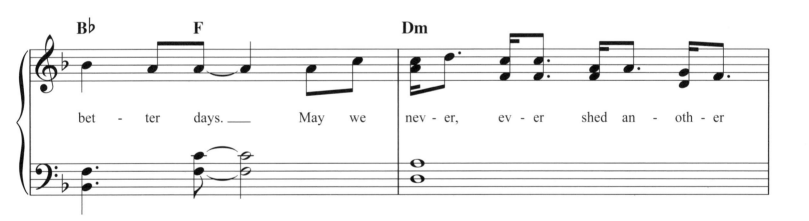

DANCE MONKEY

Words and Music by
TONI WATSON

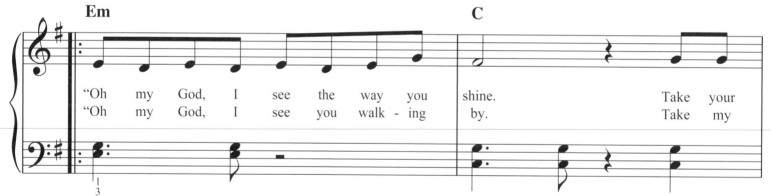

"Oh my God, I see the way you shine. Take your
"Oh my God, I see you walk-ing by. Take my

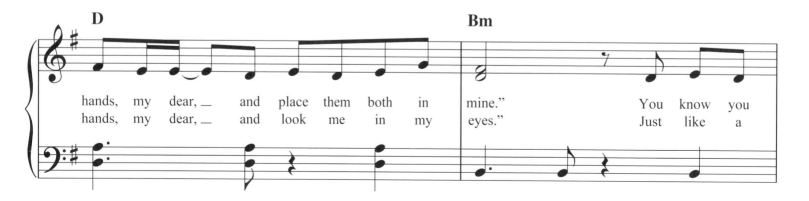

hands, my dear,___ and place them both in mine." You know you
hands, my dear,___ and look me in my eyes." Just like a

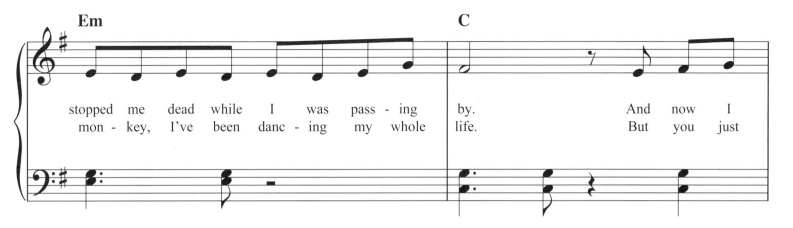

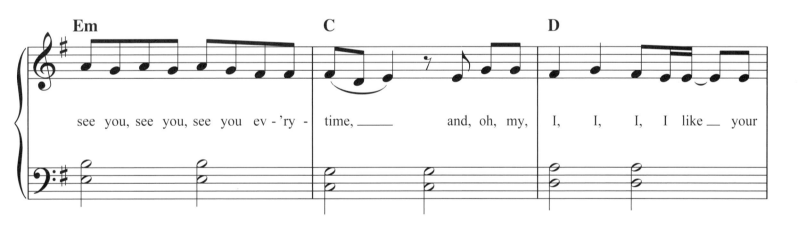

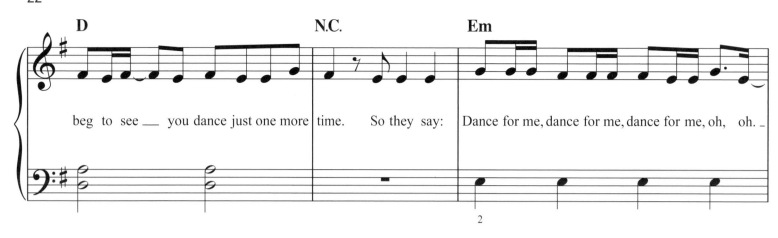

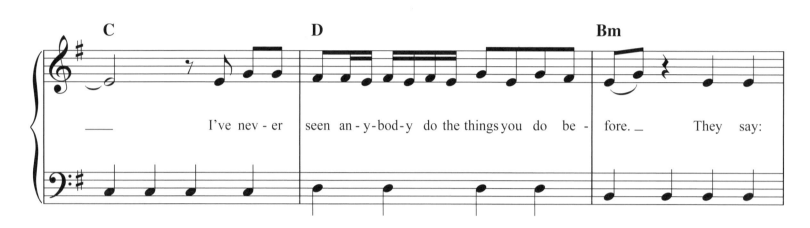

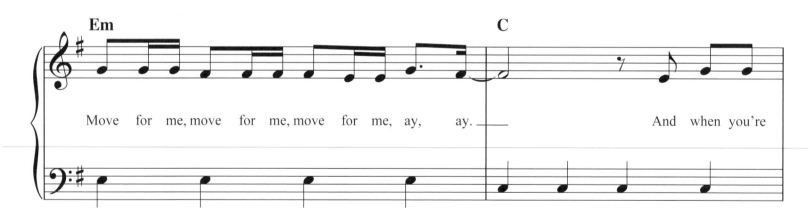

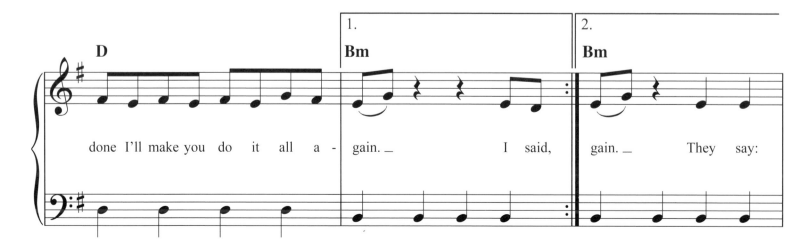

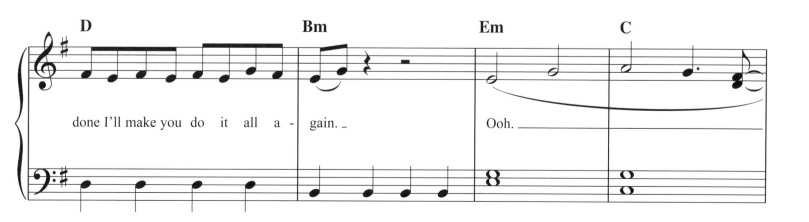

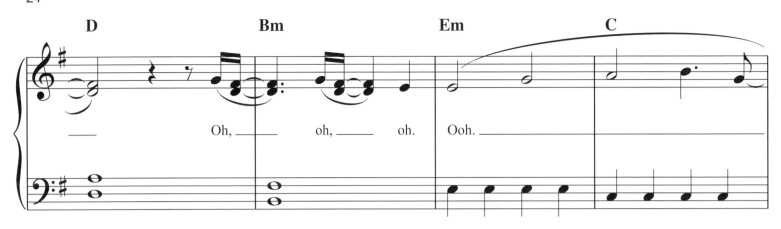

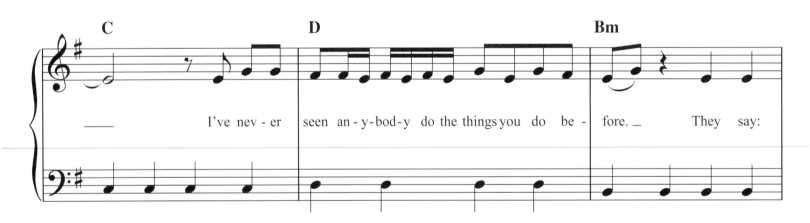

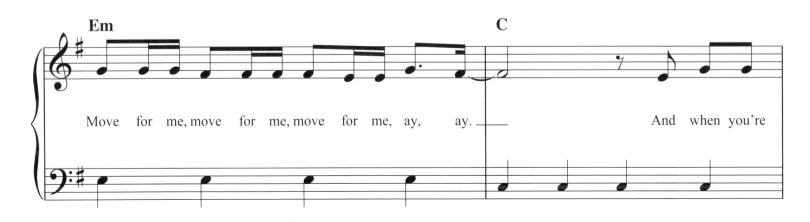

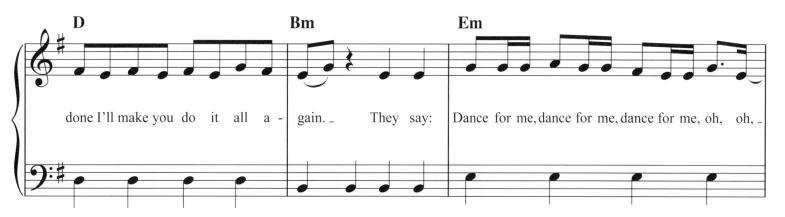

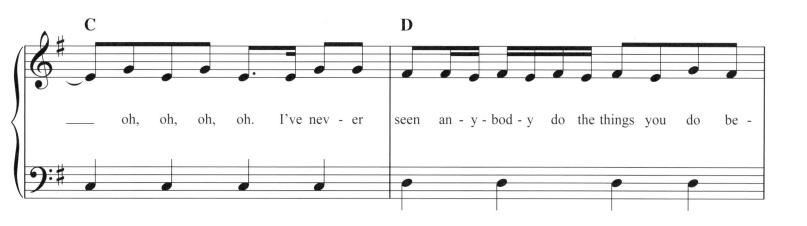

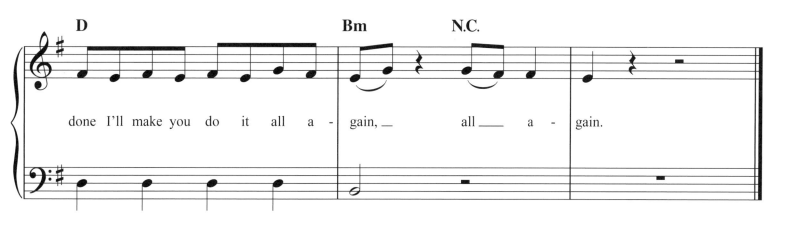

WE ARE WARRIORS
(Warrior)

Words and Music by AVRIL LAVIGNE,
CHAD KROEGER and TRAVIS CLARK

We'll pick our bat-tles 'cause we know we're gon-na win the war.
Like _ Vik-ings, we'll be fight-ing through the day and night. _

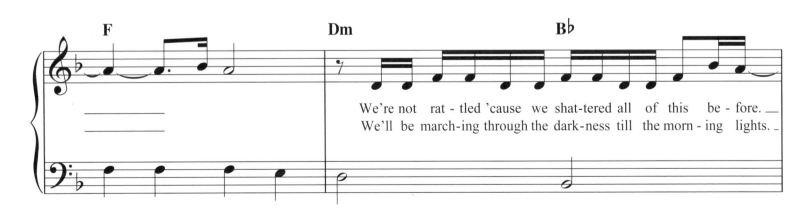

We're not rat-tled 'cause we shat-tered all of this be-fore. _
We'll be march-ing through the dark-ness till the morn-ing lights. _

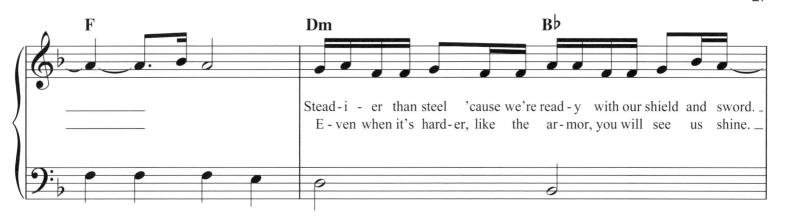

Stead-i - er than steel 'cause we're read - y with our shield and sword. _
E - ven when it's hard-er, like the ar-mor, you will see us shine. _

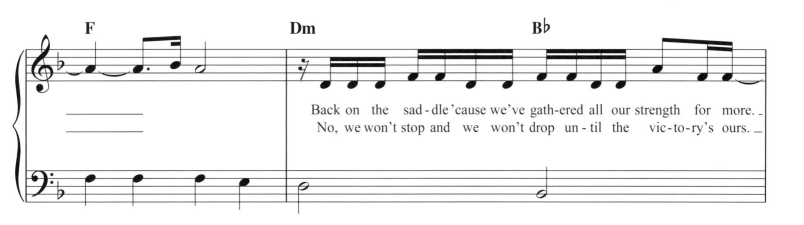

Back on the sad-dle 'cause we've gath-ered all our strength for more. _
No, we won't stop and we won't drop un - til the vic-to-ry's ours. _

And}
No,} we won't bow, we won't break.

No, we're not a-fraid to do what-ev - er it takes. We'll nev - er bow, we'll nev - er break. _

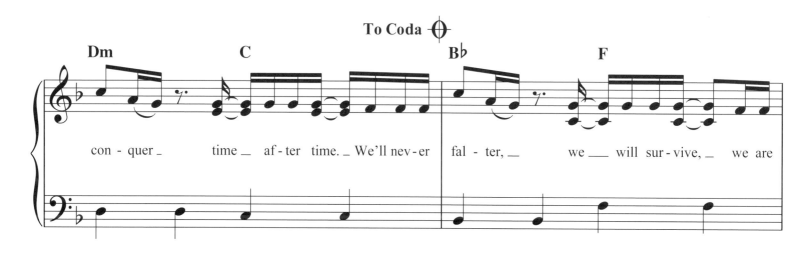

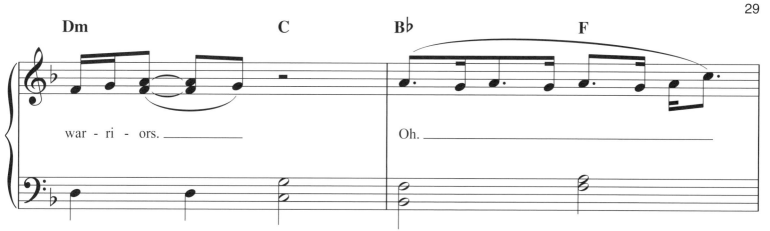

war - ri - ors. _____ Oh. _____

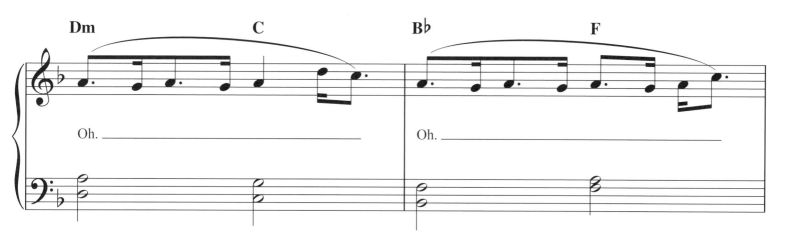

Oh. _____ Oh. _____

D.S. al Coda

We are war - ri - ors. __

CODA

fal - ter, __ we __ will sur - vive. __ We are

war - ri - ors. _____ Oh, oh, _____ you can't shoot us down. You can't

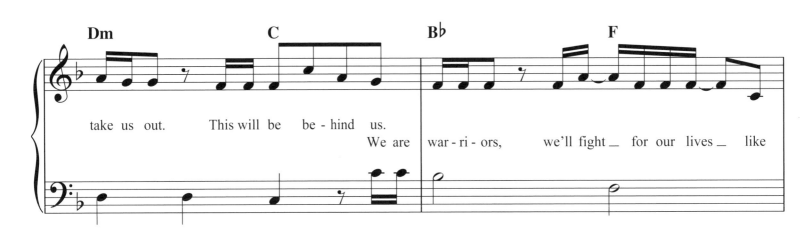

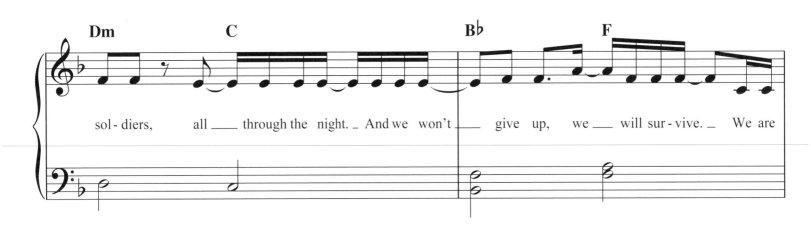

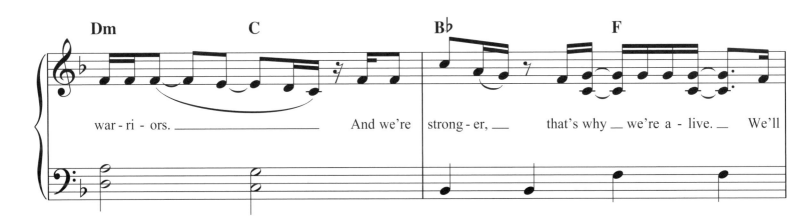

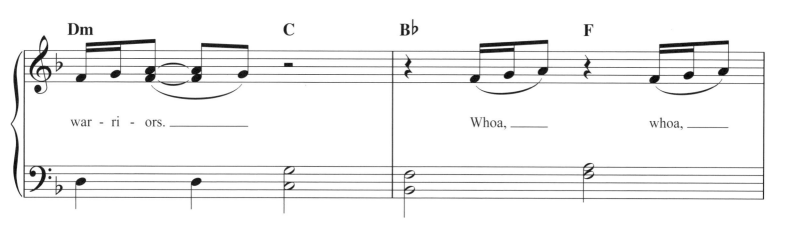

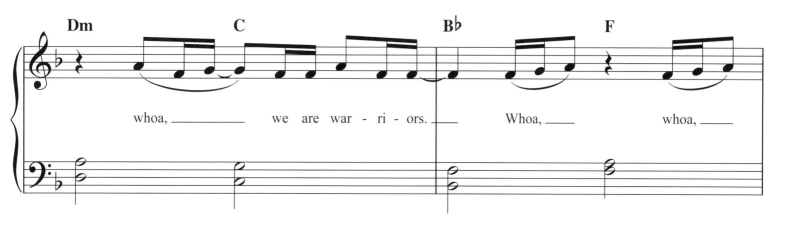

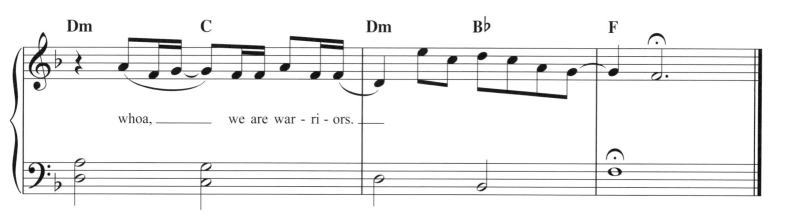

POP PIANO HITS

Pop Piano Hits is a series designed for students of all ages. Each book contains five simple and easy-to-read arrangements of today's most popular downloads. Lyrics, fingering and chord symbols are included to help you make the most of each arrangement. Enjoy your favorite songs and artists today!

BELIEVER, WHAT ABOUT US & MORE HOT SINGLES

Attention (Charlie Puth) • Believer (Imagine Dragons) • There's Nothing Holdin' Me Back (Shawn Mendes) • Too Good at Goodbyes (Sam Smith) • What About Us (P!nk).
00251934 Easy Piano $9.99

BLANK SPACE, I REALLY LIKE YOU & MORE HOT SINGLES

Blank Space (Taylor Swift) • Heartbeat Song (Kelly Clarkson) • I Really Like You (Carly Rae Jepsen) • I'm Not the Only One (Sam Smith) • Thinking Out Loud (Ed Sheeran).
00146286 Easy Piano $9.99

CAN'T STOP THE FEELING, 7 YEARS & MORE HOT SINGLES

Can't Stop the Feeling (Justin Timberlake) • H.O.L.Y. (Florida Georgia Line) • Just Like Fire (Pink) • Lost Boy (Ruth B.) • 7 Years (Lukas Graham).
00193755 Easy Piano $9.99

CITY OF STARS, MERCY & MORE HOT SINGLES

City of Stars (from *La La Land*) • Evermore (from *Beauty and the Beast*) • Mercy (Shawn Mendes) • Perfect (Ed Sheeran) • Stay (Zedd & Alessia Cara).
00236097 Easy Piano $9.99

FEEL IT STILL, REWRITE THE STARS & MORE HOT SINGLES

Feel It Still (Portugal. The Man) • Lost in Japan (Shawn Mendes) • The Middle (Zedd, Maren Morris & Grey) • Rewrite the Stars (from *The Greatest Showman*) • Whatever It Takes (Imagine Dragons).
00278090 Easy Piano $9.99

GIRLS LIKE YOU, HAPPY NOW & MORE HOT SINGLES

Girls Like You (Maroon 5) • Happy Now (Zedd feat. Elley Duhé) • Treat Myself (Meghan Trainor) • You Are the Reason (Calum Scott) • You Say (Lauren Daigle).
00285014 Easy Piano $9.99

HOW FAR I'LL GO, THIS TOWN & MORE HOT SINGLES

How Far I'll Go (Alessia Cara - from *Moana*) • My Way (Calvin Harris) • This Town (Niall Horan) • Treat You Better (Shawn Mendes) • We Don't Talk Anymore (Charlie Puth feat. Selena Gomez).
00211286 Easy Piano $9.99

I DON'T CARE, ME! & MORE HOT SINGLES

I Don't Care (Ed Sheeran & Justin Bieber) • If I Can't Have You (Shawn Mendes) • ME! (Taylor Swift) • Rainbow (Kacey Musgraves) • Someone You Loved (Lewis Capaldi).
00299798 Easy Piano $9.99

LET IT GO, HAPPY & MORE HOT SINGLES

All of Me (John Legend) • Dark Horse (Katy Perry) • Happy (Pharrell) • Let It Go (Demi Lovato) • Pompeii (Bastille).
00128204 Easy Piano $9.99

LOVE YOURSELF, STITCHES & MORE HOT SINGLES

Like I'm Gonna Lose You (Meghan Trainor) • Love Yourself (Justin Bieber) • One Call Away (Charlie Puth) • Stitches (Shawn Mendes) • Stressed Out (Twenty One Pilots).
00159285 Easy Piano $9.99

HAL•LEONARD®

www.halleonard.com

Prices, contents and availability subject to change without notice.

MEMORIES, TRUTH HURTS & MORE HOT SINGLES

Beautiful People • Lose You to Love Me • Memories • 10,000 Hours • Truth Hurts.
00328173 Easy Piano $9.99

ROAR, ROYALS & MORE HOT SINGLES

Atlas (Coldplay – from *The Hunger Games: Catching Fire*) • Roar (Katy Perry) • Royals (Lorde) • Safe and Sound (Capital Cities) • Wake Me Up! (Avicii).
00123868 Easy Piano $9.99

SAY SOMETHING, COUNTING STARS & MORE HOT SINGLES

Counting Stars (One Republic) • Demons (Imagine Dragons) • Let Her Go (Passenger) • Say Something (A Great Big World) • Story of My Life (One Direction).
00125356 Easy Piano $9.99

SEE YOU AGAIN, FLASHLIGHT & MORE HOT SINGLES

Budapest (George Ezra) • Flashlight (Jessie J.) • Honey I'm Good (Andy Grammer) • See You Again (Wiz Khalifa) • Shut Up and Dance (Walk the Moon).
00150045 Easy Piano $9.99

SHAKE IT OFF, ALL ABOUT THAT BASS & MORE HOT SINGLES

All About That Bass (Meghan Trainor) • Shake It Off (Taylor Swift) • A Sky Full of Stars (Coldplay) • Something in the Water (Carrie Underwood) • Take Me to Church (Hozier).
00142734 Easy Piano $9.99

SUNFLOWER, WITHOUT ME & MORE HOT SINGLES

High Hopes (Panic! at the Disco) • No Place (Backstreet Boys) • Shallow (Lady Gaga and Bradley Cooper) • Sunflower (Post Malone) • Without Me (Halsey).
00291634 Easy Piano $9.99

0220
186